Copyright © 2024 Grow Grit Press LLC. All rights reserved. No part of this book may be reproduced in any form without permission in writing from the publisher. Please send bulk order requests to info@ninjalifehacks.tv

Paperback ISBN: 978-1-63731-981-9
Hardcover ISBN: 978-1-63731-983-3
eBook ISBN: 978-1-63731-982-6

Printed and bound in the USA.
NinjaLifeHacks.tv

Tonight, I embark on a quest
To reveal a secret so bright.
I've heard that unicorns hide
A skill they keep out of sight.

With a key that **sparkles** in moonlight,
I sneak to a meadow so grand.
The grass whispers softly beneath my feet,
As I approach their magical land.

But as I watch, a sight unfolds,
They trip and tumble with flair.
Legs tangled in a FUNNY dance,
Hooves flying through the air.

She whispers softly, "I can run fast,"
Her heart fired with **FIERCE** ambition.
With every breath, her worries fade,
Facing the world with a bold new vision.

A unicorn sees my STRUGGLE
And offers a helping hoof.
She uses her horn to summon a breeze,
Revealing the key under a roof.

As dawn breaks, I wave goodbye
To my newfound unicorn **friends**.
They leap and run gracefully
As a magical night ends.

I love to hear from my readers. Email me your feedback or thoughts on what my next story should be at info@ninjalifehacks.tv

Yours truly, Mary

 @marynhin @GrowGrit #NinjaLifeHacks

 Mary Nhin   Ninja Life Hacks

 Ninja Life Hacks

 @officialninjalifehacks

www.ingramcontent.com/pod-product-compliance
Lightning Source LLC
Chambersburg PA
CBRC091453160426
43209CB00024B/1888